better together*

*This book is best read together, grownup and kid.

 akidsco.com

a kids book about

a kids book about

IMAGINATION

by LeVar Burton

a
kids
book
about

A Kids Book About books are available online: *akidsco.com*

To share your stories, ask questions, or inquire about bulk purchases (schools, libraries, and nonprofits), please use the following email address: *hello@akidsco.com*

ISBN: 978-1-953955-44-9

Designed by Duke Stebbins
Edited by Denise Morales Soto

I dedicate this book to the dreamer
who lives in us all.

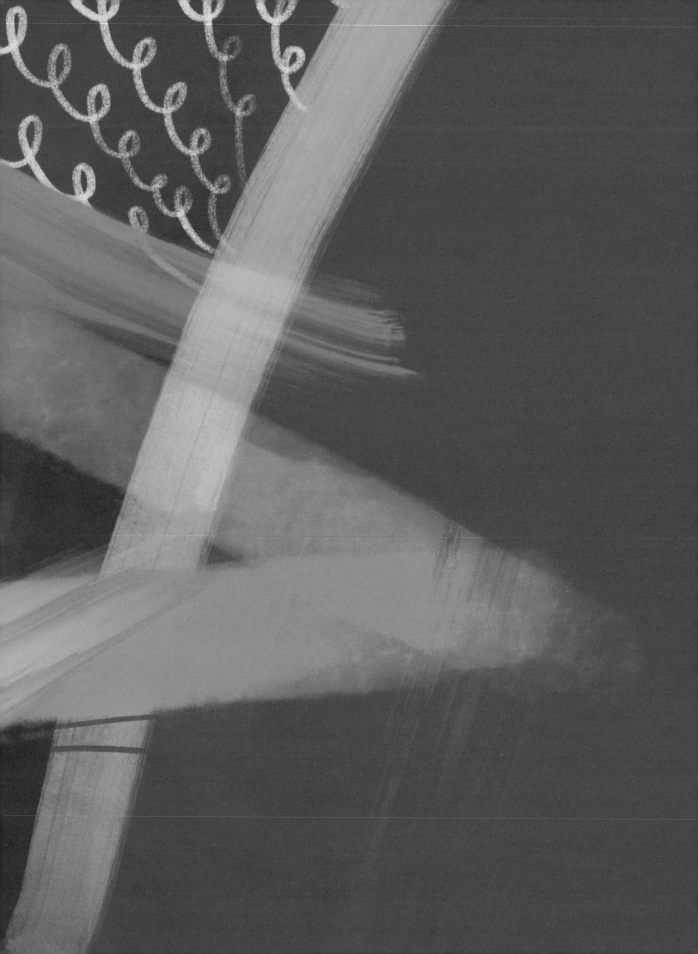

Intro

It's critical we develop a healthy relationship with our imagination. The older we get, the less we tend to exercise it. That's one of the reasons I wanted to write this book—to ignite curiosity, foster empathy, and promote a healthy exercising of our imaginations from an early age.

This upcoming generation will inherit the problems and injustices the previous ones failed to solve. It will be incumbent upon them to solve these problems, and chief among the tools they will need to do so is their imagination.

You see, our imagination is the most powerful thing we have. It allows us to visualize the possibility of *what if.*

So, as you read this book with your future changemaker, do yourself a favor and exercise your own imagination muscle. Just imagine the conversations you'll have after you've shared this together.

heroes.

How about you?

The reason I love superheroes is because they have the power to change the world and make it a better place.

But I've learned that you don't have to be a superhero to change the world.

In fact, I believe every human being

has a superpower...

I know this because
I've been to the future
and I've been to the past.*

*Just ask your grownup, they might
know what I'm talking about.

I've lived countless lives
through my many roles.

I've been enslaved on a plantation in Georgia in the 1860s.

I've explored the galaxy in a starship with an intrepid* crew.

I've read stories to millions of children all over the world.

*Intrepid means to be bold, brave, and adventurous.

All because of my imagination.

My name is LeVar and
I'm an actor, writer,
director, podcaster,
and most importantly,

a story-
teller.

And everywhere I go I ask one question with two of the most powerful words in the world: "what if?"

Asking what if
is all about possibility...

What if frogs could fly?

What if homework was optional?

What if I was loved or accepted just the way I am?

When I ask what if,
I use my superpower,

imagination.

Imagination is the power
to dream up the world
the way you'd like it to be.

Thinking up not just what is,
but what could be.

I didn't find this superpower on my own.

My mother Erma Gene
was an avid* reader.

She introduced me to
the world of books.

*Avid means to be eager and enthusiastic.

In books, I found
companionship, adventure,
magic, and inspiration.

Even though they were just filled with words, books are also full of entire universes.

They helped me see the world as a place where I belonged.

They made me more

empow
—ered.

They made me more

courag
eous.

They also made me feel less alone.

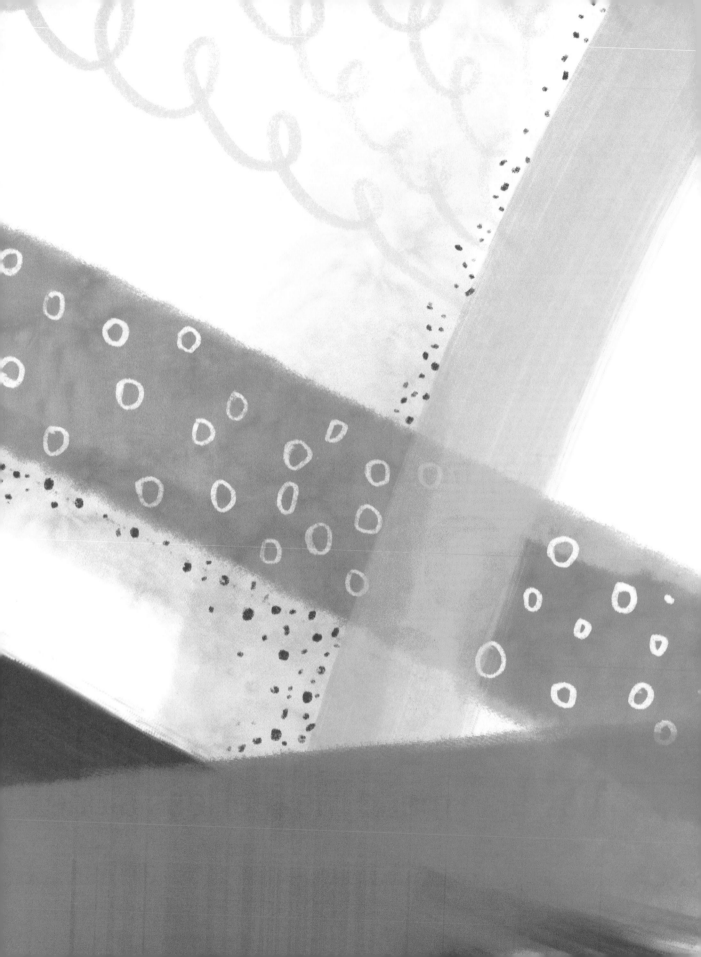

Imagine all that from just a book!
But that's how imagination works.

Imagination is a tool for

change.

Imagination is the machine we use to

invent.

Imagination is our creative self in

action.

We can imagine ourselves in the past, present, and future, and no other species on earth can do that.

Now, you might think you **aren't any good** at using your imagination.

But one of the best things about our imagination is that we are using it all the time, even if we aren't aware of it.

Do you think about what or who you'll be when you grow up?

Do you watch TV and wish you were one of the lead characters?

Have you ever considered how things might have gone had you made a different decision?

You have?

Well, you're using your imagination!

Now, here's the important part:

Imagination is a muscle.

While we're all born with it,
did you know that you
can strengthen it?

Flex your
imagination by

bigger and
brighter futures.

about everything.

Don't accept things as is.

Think of how they COULD BE.

Tell stories how you wish they were told, not simply how they've been given.

Think of the possibilities when asking,

what if?

Imagination is SO important!

Everything made by people is the product of imagination.

Every great movement started with someone using their imagination.

Every great invention is created by someone using their imagination.

Every great problem is solved by someone using their imagination.

When we don't use our imagination...

we actually limit the possibilities that exist in our world.

Yes, you, the kid reading this book.

Your imagination is more powerful

than you think.

So use your superpower
and ask what if?

What if you lived in a world
that was fair for everyone?

What if prejudice or racism
didn't exist?

What if everyone you cared about felt safe and loved?

What if every kid felt
like they belonged?

What if everyone, everywhere had what they needed to survive?

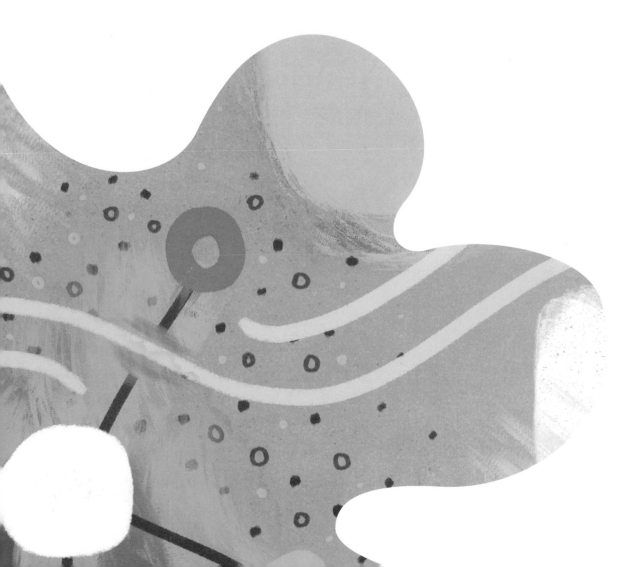

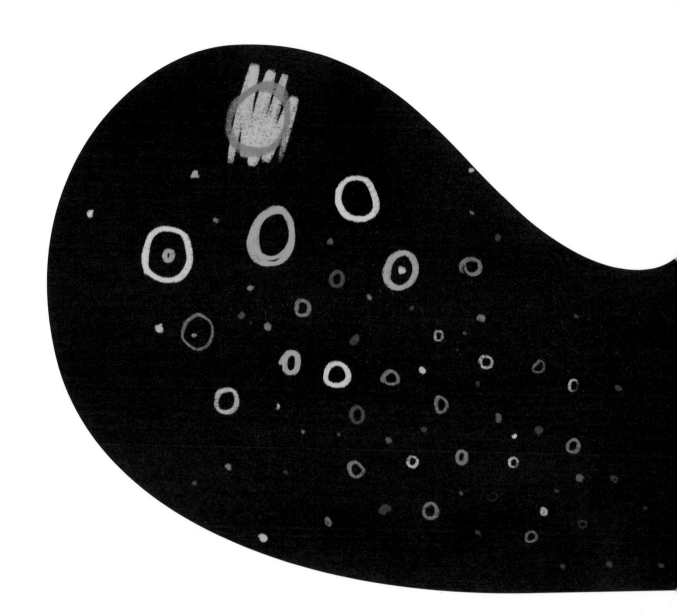

What if the universe had in store for you something bigger, better, and greater than anything you could ever imagine for yourself?

Just imagine—

what if...?

Outro

Now that we've unlocked our innate superpower, my hope is you will actively engage in the development and strengthening of your kid's imagination muscle—today, tomorrow, and well into their adult lives.

Encourage them to never stop asking, "What if?" And when they do, don't be afraid to engage in the process along with them.

Our imaginations reinforce the possibility of the universe...and the possibilities are endless.

But you don't have to take my word for it.

find more kids books about

belonging, feminism, identity, money, leadership, racism, gratitude, body image, boredom, creativity, and climate change.

a akidsco.com

notes

share
your read*

*Tell somebody, post a photo, or give this book away to share what you care about.

 **@akidsco**